04/19

D0403001

JULIET'S

School

— OF —

Possibilities

JULIET'S

School

— OF —

Possibilities

A Little Story About the Power of Priorities

Laura Vanderkam

PORTFOLIO / PENGUIN

Portfolio/Penguin
An imprint of Penguin Random House LLC
penguinrandomhouse.com

Most Portfolio books are available at a discount when purchased in quantity
for sales promotions or corporate use. Special editions, which include personalized
covers, excerpts, and corporate imprints, can be created when purchased
in large quantities. For more information, please call (212) 572–2232 or
e-mail specialmarkets@penguinrandomhouse.com. Your local bookstore can
also assist with discounted bulk purchases using the Penguin Random House
corporate Business-to-Business program. For assistance in locating a participating
retailer, e-mail B2B@penguinrandomhouse.com.

LIBRARY OF CONGRESS CATALOGING-IN-PUBLICATION DATA
Names: Vanderkam, Laura, author.
Title: Juliet's school of possibilities : a little story about
the power of priorities / Laura Vanderkam.
Description: New York : Portfolio/Penguin, [2019] |
Identifiers: LCCN 2018045725 (print) | LCCN 2018047875 (ebook) |
ISBN 9780525538950 (ebook) | ISBN 9780525538943 (hardcover)
Subjects: LCSH: Women--Vocational guidance. |
Success. | Self-realization. | Vocation.
Classification: LCC HF5382.6 (ebook) | LCC HF5382.6 .V36 2019 (print) |
DDC 650.1082--dc23
LC record available at https://lccn.loc.gov/2018045725

Printed in the United States of America
1   3   5   7   9   10   8   6   4   2

Book design by Cassandra Garruzzo

Contents

JULIET'S

School

— OF —

Possibilities

Chapter 1

Ctober's red and gold leaves blazed bright as Riley Jenkins drove south along the Garden State Parkway. *Lovely enough,* she thought, but even the fall colors failed to lift her mood. Nor could she summon the energy to be excited about her destination: her firm's women's leadership retreat in the little town of Maris, along the New Jersey coast.

It wasn't that she resented working on a Saturday. Riley couldn't think of a Saturday she hadn't worked since landing her job with MB & Company, the consulting firm, after earning her Wharton M.B.A. four years before.

No, it was the opportunity cost of spending her Saturday with *colleagues* when she should be finding *clients*.

After all, it was clients who got you ahead at MB, the most elite of all firms. It was clients who gave you power at this place she had long wanted to work. She remembered learning of its mystique in a casual conversation with a professor years ago, back when she'd been an undergrad at Indiana University and waitressing to cover costs that her scholarship didn't. MB let you work with CEOs. Prime ministers. You could solve their most important challenges and hence impact the world at a scale few other careers allowed. It didn't matter if you weren't yet thirty years old. You could earn copious cash while jetting around the world—in her first year, double what her staid Midwestern parents earned, combined, at their peak. Stick it out to partner and you'd take home millions.

Riley prided herself on responding to clients as close to instantly as possible. In her four-year rise from star hire through project manager to an associate partner, she had rarely made clients wait more than an hour. She set up her phone to let her know when they emailed as she drove her rental cars around (having grown up as a small-town Indiana girl, she still felt strange about hiring drivers). Her assistant knew not to book her on flights that didn't have internet access.

But then . . . Her mind zipped back to last week's show-down with her evaluator. Jean had guided her into that horrible beige conference room in the NYC office that she saw—thankfully—only when she wasn't at client sites. "Riley," she had begun. The older woman had kept taking her glasses off and rubbing her eyes. Riley soon understood why Jean was dreading this conversation. Riley was being put in the "Challenges" bucket in MB's elaborate rating system. It was below "Average" and only one step above "Resignation Suggested." (MB was too genteel to ever *demand* a resignation or, the height of tawdriness, actually *fire* someone.)

Riley played the scene over and over in her mind as the exit numbers on the Garden State Parkway ticked down. "I have never been below average in my life," she told Jean.

"Well, it's 'Challenges' for MB," Jean had said. "That doesn't mean you wouldn't be excellent somewhere else."

Was that a threat? Riley didn't want to go anywhere else. She'd wanted to be an MB consultant with the same zeal with which her college roommate and best friend Skip had wanted to protest drone strikes. She couldn't imagine anywhere else offering this pace, this variety, and yes, this paycheck.

"I don't get it," Riley had said. "I do everything the clients want. I get them just what they ask for faster than they expect it."

"Yes, yes." Jean had looked around that beige conference room, as if she thought someone might be spying on them. Then she lowered her voice. "Listen, Riley. Here's the thing. You're four years in. Newly in leadership. Everyone I interviewed said you're floundering in the role."

"But I'm . . ." She had started to protest. Floundering? Riley Jenkins did not flounder at *anything*.

"Riley, listen to me. I am trying to help you here. Your upward feedback in particular was terrible. Your team members say you're so unfocused and distracted that they work around the clock, but they never know if they're working on the right things. Look—up until now you could just do what the partners told you to. Which you did." She had taken her glasses off again and searched for the right image. Finally: "You're like the world's most powerful drill. Point you at something and you drill a hole instantly."

"Um, OK."

"But at this level you need to think about where the drill should go. And frankly, your clients and your colleagues don't see insight there. You need big ideas. Ideas your teams get excited about. Ideas the clients haven't even imagined. Ideas that you can suggest—so then they have to hire MB, right?"

"I see," Riley had said.

"It's about the business case, Riley. Making partner is about being able to sell big ideas." Jean had suddenly glanced around, worried. "Sorry, convince people that they need to engage MB to study your ideas. We don't use the word 'sell' around here."

"Of course." That strange MB fussiness. "I will work on that."

"Yes," she said. "Please do." She sighed. "Being in 'Challenges' means I need to document every thirty days that you are making real progress. If you are not, that's when other ratings come into play."

Riley had said nothing. Jean played her cards close, like the big players in the casino where Riley worked one summer years before, but she knew what this meant. If she hadn't made a sale in thirty days, she was out.

That had been a little over a week ago. The truth is, she had no idea how she was going to find space for brilliance. She couldn't *not* do what her clients and colleagues asked, and their demands already filled every available minute. They filled minutes that weren't available. She had been up so late the past few nights working on a proposal for her major client, a chain of extraordinarily hip cafés called The People's Coffee Shops (or PCS, for short), that her brain could focus on little beyond finding time for a nap.

She glanced at her phone's GPS. Fifteen miles until the turn. Thirty minutes until she would arrive at this mysterious retreat location called Juliet's School of Possibilities, owned by the eponymous domestic maven. Riley had seen Juliet's TV shows occasionally in hotels when she was too stressed to sleep. How to host the perfect bridal shower. How to decorate a living room for $100. Apparently she ran corporate retreats too. The women's leadership group of the Northeast US offices had booked a weekend there to bond over cooking, crafts, and bike rides along the boardwalk.

Riley wasn't sure how welcome she was. Nadia, a power player in the New York office, had said it was going to be just partners. Unfortunately, there were so few female partners at MB that they needed to dip down a level on the ladder to fill the retreat center and thus have the place to themselves. Riley—miffed at this—added it in as a reason not to go, along with a vague sense that she hadn't seen her boyfriend, Neil, in a while. A week? No, two . . . *three*? It didn't seem possible that time had sped by so much since their last date—pints at a beer garden, with Riley feeling more energized by every round of conversation with the brilliant entrepreneur. He had invited her to come meet his extended family soon. She had started daydreaming about Thanksgiving.

Then Elsa, the chief marketing officer at PCS, mentioned being a fan of Juliet. Elsa moonlighted as a supermom to three boys in whatever time she wasn't shining a spotlight on the farmer who'd grown the wheat used in PCS scones. She proclaimed her jealousy that Riley got to go. It was the nicest thing Elsa had said to her the entire previous weekend. Riley and team had been cooped up with her for a miserable two days in another beige conference room, the weekend meeting happening because Elsa's husband and their boys were off camping with the Cub Scouts. Elsa had to meet with her CEO soon. Elsa had asked for ideas to bring to him. The team had flailed around in different directions all the following week before frantically cranking out a proposal to get it in by 9 p.m. Friday. This was right after Elsa's children went to bed, and hence when she looked at things. She wrapped up her emails by 11 p.m. That they hadn't heard anything by Saturday midday wasn't a good sign.

After a few more minutes of stewing—*we must see progress*

in thirty days—Riley couldn't help herself. She dialed the manager on the proposed project. "Hey, Frank, it's Riley," she said. "You haven't heard from Elsa, have you?"

"Oh, hey," Frank said. He sounded like he'd just woken up. "I hadn't checked email yet this morning." Riley seethed. It was almost noon. How irresponsible was that? "Let me look . . . Oh."

"Oh?"

"Not good. She's reaching out to other consulting firms. This isn't what she's looking for."

Riley grabbed the second phone she kept so she could look at email while running other apps on her first phone. She spotted an emergency pull-off spot—this was definitely an emergency—and swerved slightly as she eased over to hunt through her inbox. She perched the phone on top of the wheel and scrolled down. "How could I miss that?"

"Strange—I don't think you're copied. Well, too bad. But Steve—you know Steve? He's amazing to work with. He's likely getting some projects in another part of PCS. So we win some, we lose some . . ."

Riley gripped the wheel as she drove back onto the highway. *But I can't lose some right now,* she thought. She had three weeks. "OK, thanks for letting me know." She could not keep the sarcasm out of her voice.

As she signaled to pass a truck lumbering in front of her, she let out her breath slowly. Riley was not an emotional person. But she . . . *liked* Elsa. Admired her. Why hadn't she even copied her? Had Riley misread so much? She glanced at her phone. It was a Saturday. It was presumptuous to call a client on a weekend. But she had to know.

"Hello?" the woman answered after three rings.

"Elsa? This is Riley. From MB."

"Oh." Riley could hear the noise of a soccer game in the background.

"Can you talk now?"

"Not for long. Robbie's playing goalie."

She plunged in. "I just heard from Frank that you were reaching out to other consulting firms about ideas to take to Jacob."

"Yes, well . . ." Elsa shouted something at a child on the field. "To be honest, the proposal you sent me was just . . . how shall I put this? Amateur."

Riley had to hit her brakes as a Prius cut in front of her. "I'm sorry—did you say *amateur*?"

"It's like you put no original thought into it whatsoever. If I wanted to write the damn thing myself, I would have done that."

"We spent all last weekend talking about what you wanted . . ."

"And clearly you weren't listening. I can't say I'm surprised. You were looking at your phone the whole time. And then trying to listen in to a conference call with your *travel department* while I was talking to you."

"I . . ." Riley tried to remember. She had been sorting out a blowup about a client in Atlanta and a colleague's continual questions about the logistics of a meeting in London that never happened. She was about to apologize, but Elsa interrupted her.

"Look, if that represents your best thinking, I don't see why we need to keep working together." She paused. Riley supposed Elsa recognized how harsh that sounded. Her Cub Scout mom side now needed to smooth things over. Her voice softened. "Say, are you on the way to Juliet's School of Possibilities?"

"According to my map, I'm twenty minutes away."

"Delightful. Such a fascinating woman. Are you going to meet her? I assume she has other people do the retreats . . ."

"One of my colleagues knows her, so she's going to at least say hello."

"I just watched her fall food and decorating special. I made her acorn squash harvest bowls with pomegranate arils, and I shellacked these yellow leaves to make a wreath for my door. I'll send you a picture, OK? *Robbie—watch the ball! Don't let them—hey! Out to John! Yes!!!! Good hustle!* Riley, I gotta go . . ."

And she was gone.

Riley clenched her teeth. *Amateur.* How had this happened? Could things get any worse?

What a question. Of course they could.

Chapter 2

———————

Her phone rang before she managed to cut back into the right lane. Neil. As the call log popped up—it seemed he'd tried her several times in the last twenty-four hours—she remembered: They *had* in fact made plans for that night. She recalled a flurry of emails on Tuesday, or possibly Thursday. Her mind ransacked the mess of her calendar. Dinner? A movie? In the rush of concocting that doomed proposal for Elsa, she realized, she hadn't told him that she was going to the retreat instead of staying in the city to work.

She supposed she needed to tell him now. "Hey, Neil," she said. "I'm really glad to hear your voice." It was true. He was a calm presence amid the MB frenzy—the only person she'd dared confide in, albeit by text message, about her dismal performance review. "I saw you called and I meant to call you earlier but . . ."

"I'm glad to hear your voice because it means you actually picked up the phone." He spoke carefully—like Jean in that conference room, as she thought about it—but his voice had an edge. It wasn't a tone Riley had heard from him before. She felt her stomach clench with an unease about where this conversation was headed.

She tried to compose herself. "I'm sorry. I've just been so busy. My horrible evaluation has got me . . ."

"You know I'm busy too. Everyone's busy, Riley."

"Neil . . ." Something was definitely wrong. What had she done? She recalled from one of his messages that he'd just closed a second round of funding for his health data app, a thought that suddenly pained Riley; he had wanted to get together that night to toast the accomplishment, but she'd said she didn't have time. Was that it? She thought back to another toast—the April night they'd met. He had struck up a conversation with her at a bar where she was celebrating with her MB colleagues after winning a project with a major retail chain. The client had contracted for months of work. She was giddy with the promise of it—even more when this handsome and cerebral man had introduced himself. Rather than getting her number and texting to ask her out, he'd simply asked her to dinner the next night. In person. Did people even do that anymore?

Then her mind whirled to all that had failed in implementation. Of the retail work and with her attempts to spend time with Neil too. *Challenges*.

"Yet oddly, I manage to pick up when you call. And I show up when we have plans."

"I'm so sorry." How many times could she say that? "I meant to tell you . . . I really want to see you, but I'm actually on the way to Maris on the Jersey Shore for that retreat I told you about. I was crashing on a proposal and I just forgot I hadn't told you . . ."

"Oh, you're canceling our plans tonight too? I was talking about *last* night."

"Last night? What are you talking about?" He must have emailed her; she must have lost the note amid everything else. "We were supposed to go out last night?"

"Remember, I got tickets for that Chekhov play. You said you wanted to go. So, since I respect your time and care about you, I wrapped up my work in time to meet you there. I tried calling you several times, but I figured out by intermission that you weren't coming. At least I got to see the second half."

And as he was sitting outside the theater by himself, Riley thought, she had been juggling two conference calls that achieved nothing and frantically finishing a proposal Elsa wanted nothing to do with. "Neil, I'm—I just had to work and . . ."

"You don't *have* to do anything, Riley. You don't have to leap at whatever is blinking in front of you. You don't have to rip up everything for whatever seems urgent." He coughed. Then, methodically, the blow: "Waiting for you last night gave me some time to think. I realized that while you are an absolutely amazing woman, I am not interested in being treated like this. A satisfying relationship requires a certain quantity of time and respect for the other person. Neither of which seems to be a priority for you at the moment."

Riley caught her breath. "Are you . . . breaking up with me?"

"I guess that's what it is. I wish we could have this conversation in person, but you keep canceling our plans. Or not showing up. Of course, if I was able to talk with you in person, we *wouldn't* be having this conversation . . ."

"Neil . . ."

"Trust me, I'm not happy about it. But we're not twenty years old. It's not fair to you or me to string this along if it's not going anywhere."

"I didn't think it wasn't going anywhere." In a moment, the various semi-plans Riley had daydreamed about dissipated. Future vacations. Idly looking at real estate listings together. This destruction of her envisioned future was so disorienting she felt more shocked than sad. "We'd talked about visiting your parents for Thanksgiving . . ."

"And you and I both know you'd get a request for a proposal from a European client that would be due on Friday, since they don't celebrate Thanksgiving, and you'd cancel your plans to meet my family for that." Riley didn't answer. Was this a hypothetical? The truth is, she had done just that to her last boyfriend the Thanksgiving before. Did Neil know about that? Did *Skip* tell him? The idea that her best friend might be warning people about her history shot Riley down a rabbit hole of worry. Then, as with Elsa, she noticed Neil's voice softening. "Enjoy your retreat, OK? Try to relax. I think you could use it."

And then he was gone too. Riley bit her lip. She clenched

her fists and tried to keep calm as Neil's curt words—and Elsa's as well—whirled around in her mind. How was this possible? Was there *anyone* important in her life that she wasn't disappointing?

As if on cue, her phone rang again. Skip. Riley's voice shook as she told her phone to answer. Since they'd met as freshmen at IU—a strange late-night encounter after Riley used the dorm fire extinguisher to douse a blaze caused by some idiot putting a cigarette in the recycling bin—they'd been close. Skip had always been the idealistic one. After a few miserable years in corporate communications, she had started a nonprofit serving middle school girls in a not-yet-gentrified corner of Brooklyn. Almost overnight, she was reawakened to life, even if the work itself was keep-you-up-all-night stressful. Riley wanted to be a good friend to Skip. She wanted to listen when Skip called in tears because one of her girls did some stupid teenage thing, and because the world gave these girls few breaks, a promising life would now be marked. But there was always something else to do. She would be on the phone making encouraging noises to Skip, and she'd be deleting emails as they came in.

As Riley heard Skip's voice, she realized that *yes,* there was one more person to disappoint.

"Hi, Skip, I . . ."

"Listen, Riley, we've got to talk. I was trying you all yesterday."

"I know, I know . . . I'm sorry I didn't return your call. My team was working all day to get this proposal in and . . ."

"Riley, I've been trying to get you all *week*. I told you— I have a meeting with this potential funder early next week. I can't say who, but it would be a huge corporate connection."

"That's great, Skip . . ."

"Yeah—I met her at that party a few months ago. That NYC parks benefit I convinced my old boss to give us tickets for? You left early to fly to Frankfurt—remember? That was that meeting you found out was canceled while you were taxiing on the runway . . ."

"Yes, Skip, I remember." Even worse: It had been an internal meeting. That part of the MB lifestyle seldom made it into the recruiting pitches.

"She said she only wants to fund something innovative. I thought you were going to talk through ideas with me."

"Yes, I planned to and . . ."

"And your assistant—not you, your *assistant*—called me to cancel lunch on Friday." Her voice was even angrier than Elsa's.

"Skip . . ." Now Riley could feel the tears she had managed not to start shedding with Neil. "I so wanted to meet you—Oh, Skip, you have great ideas anyway. You don't need me . . ."

"Well, I have ideas, but I need help making the numbers look like someone with an MBA has thought through them."

"Skip, I'm sorry, I can't do anything right. Neil just called."

"Oh . . ."

Riley was slightly ashamed of this transparent attempt to shift the conversation. Skip couldn't stay furious if Riley was miserable, could she? She glanced in the rearview mirror at her red eyes and smearing makeup. "He broke up with me."

"He did? By *phone*?"

"Because I forgot I had plans with him last night. Can you believe that?"

Silence. Riley imagined that Skip could hear her anguish, and wanted to console her about being dumped. But on the other hand, her own anger simmered, and was about to bubble over. "Well . . . I'm sorry if this sounds harsh, but *yes,* I can believe that."

"Skip!"

"He's a great guy. I know I'm your friend but . . . nobody has infinite patience."

"Skip." That hurt. "Well, to seal my fate, I hadn't mentioned I was gone today with that retreat I told you about. You know, Juliet's School of Possibilities? On the Jersey Shore?"

"Your retreat . . . So you're not coming over to help me think about ideas now, are you?"

"I have the next fifteen minutes by phone. Wait, did I miss my turn?"

"Forget it, Riley. You're busy." Skip coughed. "I'll figure something out. I'm just . . ." She paused. "I value our friendship. I'm also upset that I seem to be so low on the priority list for you."

"You're not low on the list, it's just . . ." But there was no other way to explain it, and now nothing she could do except watch her GPS recalculate a route through the back roads toward the beach. She drove through swampland, cedars, and over a stone bridge next to a historic courthouse ringed by a fence covered in crimson vines. The leaves blazed even brighter here off the highway. In the distance, a white lighthouse shone against a small grove of poplars. This fall glory commanded Riley's attention. She pulled over, grabbed her phone, and snapped a few photos of the lighthouse and the trees. For a moment she forgot everything weighing on her.

But only for a moment. She looked at her inbox—356 unread messages. The familiar knot in her stomach tightened. And then this thought: *How could she be so in demand from people she didn't care about when the people she actually liked had given up on her?*

Chapter 3

J uliet's School of Possibilities rose one level above the
other Victorian houses of Maris—a reminder of the
grand inn it used to be. Once, this little town on
the Jersey Shore lured streams of vacationers on the train from
New York. They would disembark at the station a mile and a
half inland and take waiting carriages to the beach, passing
homes with stately porches. As with all places inhabited for
centuries, the town's popularity rose and fell. Now, holiday
seekers could fly direct to Miami. The old hotels had become
condos, or had succumbed to weather. But Juliet's school had

been restored and lovingly cared for, its red and white siding, its stone trim and garrets beckoning the traveler in. As Riley showed the guard her ID and pulled into the parking area—mostly empty, due to her colleagues' car service habits—she counted numerous porches offering their own possibilities for daydreaming. A giant wraparound porch on the main level sported tables and rocking chairs. A balcony on the second floor offered observers an unobstructed view of the waves. Then she spotted tiny balconies among the eaves on the third floor, perhaps off the rooms where visitors stayed while visiting Juliet.

Riley was more curious about the crafts and cooking maven than she was willing to admit. During the last ten minutes of the drive, she had her phone read her Juliet's Wikipedia entry. Maybe it was to distract herself from her misery. Or maybe, she thought, the knowledge might help her get back in with Elsa. She and Riley could shellack leaf wreaths together, as her older male colleagues golfed with their clients.

Juliet's domestic empire, the phone had intoned, was as concocted from scratch as her baked goods. Her only professional training had been a gig at an inn in western Pennsylvania years before. After she began working there, the hotel garnered glowing coverage in travel magazines, and even a nod from a notoriously cantankerous travel critic who wrote a newsletter under a pseudonym and traveled in disguise. Juliet transitioned from that job to making videos celebrating the domestic arts. She did a Christmas special first, because everyone loved to decorate and cook for the holidays, and Juliet's marketing instinct seemed birthed on Madison Avenue, not at a small inn amid the Alleghenies. She created her recipes with Instagram in mind. People couldn't help but share pictures of their concoctions. As they credited her, her influence grew. She had two school-age daughters, Betsy and Faye, who became major characters in her brand development. One year, twenty million people cast votes on which of several homemade costumes each girl should wear for Halloween. Juliet's tutorial on creating a stunning but easy baby scrapbook had likewise been watched more times since its release than there had been babies born in the English-speaking world. She leveraged that recognition into books, her website, and of course this school, perched on the shore, offering a haven for those looking to escape their lives and indulge in all forms of the domestic arts.

There in the parking lot, Riley tried to compose herself as she studied her inbox—now 415 unread messages. She deleted obvious spam and outdated internal newsletters, but she saw few easy wins. Most messages were from real people. She took a swig of coffee from her travel mug. She needed the caffeine to be up late again, finishing all her emails, after trying to be engaged with her colleagues, trying to convince them that she was the sort of original thinker who deserved to make partner in two years, trying not to think about Neil's anger or Skip's disappointment. She stared at the school. Maybe Neil and Elsa were right, she thought; since she'd bothered to come, *I should just try to learn something.* If nothing else, maybe the food would be decent. And the wine. She might forget that her life was falling apart.

She yanked her leather duffel bag out of her trunk. She hit the locks, walked to the front door, and prepared to ring the bell.

The door opened while her hand was poised in midair.

"Welcome!" A woman's rich voice rose above the ocean's roar and the faraway sound of a train.

Riley stepped back, startled. It was Juliet herself. She recognized her immediately. Her wavy auburn hair framed her face and highlighted her gentle green eyes. She was dressed casually: jeans, black T-shirt, black cardigan for the October chill. She wasn't thin, though she certainly wasn't overweight either. It was more about being substantial. Regal. She took up enough space to be a presence. When she moved, the scent of vanilla extract floated into the air.

"I'm Juliet." The woman offered her hand.

"Riley Jenkins," Riley said, doing the same. As they shook hands she could feel a spark, an energy, emanating from her host. There was something extraordinary about the way Juliet studied her. In her eyes, Riley could see Juliet coming immediately to understandings that she herself had not. They simply stood there, holding on for a minute.

Then, finally, Juliet smiled at her. "Yes, Riley. Fabulous. The starfish room." Riley marveled. Could this woman possibly know where all her guests were staying? Riley could barely remember her own hotel room numbers. Twice in the last month she'd wandered the halls of Hyatts, calling the front desk for clues. "Bob—he runs this property—will get your bag up there. It's only your colleagues here this weekend so it will be fine." A smiling man with dark hair, a goatee, and a Juliet's School of Possibilities T-shirt swooped in to cart Riley's duffel bag into the vast building. Riley followed Juliet through the door, noting the wreath of shellacked maple and oak leaves, which framed some script she couldn't quite make out: *You are always . . .* She meant to take a photo to send to Elsa. Alas, the act of pulling out her phone forced a look at her inbox—back to 415 unread messages. She was no further than where she started.

A dozen of Riley's MB colleagues perched on purple upholstered chairs in the parlor. A fire crackled in the fireplace, casting its flickering glow on shelves of books and paintings of fruit. Riley headed toward them, but Juliet stopped her. "Can I give you a quick tour? I'd love to chat with you before your first meeting." Puzzled, Riley waved at her colleagues, then followed. She had expected one drop-in appearance, not that this woman would serve as the welcoming committee. As they walked down a hall lined with antique clocks and a framed piece of calligraphy—she squinted at the words: *infinite*?— Juliet gestured at someone in the other room. A man with curly red hair brought over a tray of mulled wine.

"Just a little something. I can see that you had a rough trip." Juliet paused and handed Riley a glass. "I love this new style you tried with the lemon zests," she told the man. He beamed.

Sure enough, each mug bore an improbably curly citrus ribbon. "Harold is our kitchen guru," Juliet said. "Nothing goes on Instagram without him."

Riley took a sip. Was her despair written so obviously on her face? The warm liquid was magically soothing. As she breathed it in, a young woman hurried past.

"Kylie," Juliet called to her. "Before I forget, please do register for that blogging conference in May. We'll sort out the coverage. I'm thrilled you want to take that on. I can definitely see you managing more of our content."

"Awesome!" Kylie said. "Betsy was looking for you—she's in the kitchen."

"She's got Rachel?" Kylie nodded. Juliet tapped the bracelet on her wrist absentmindedly. Riley saw letters stamped on the metal; she tried to make them out, but Juliet was soon repositioning a vase with a sprig of highbush blueberries. "My daughter watches Kylie's daughter, Rachel, sometimes while she's here. We use Rachel as our baby model. I did not hire Kylie as my assistant because she would produce an adorable baby, but that has been a much-appreciated bonus. Betsy!" Juliet walked into the kitchen. A few staff members bustled about chopping vegetables. "Oh, good. They've got the marinade going for the duck."

"I thought we were cooking dinner?" Riley said. In selling this retreat, Nadia had sent daily emails promising that staff chefs would teach kitchen techniques: cutting, braising, making meringues. Riley rarely graced a kitchen now, but she and Skip had taught themselves how to cook during college out of economic necessity. "I was looking forward to improving my knife skills."

Juliet turned to her, assessed if she was serious, then decided she was. "I will apprentice you to Kevin. You will leave here chopping onions that will make people weep by their uniform beauty alone." Then she leaned in to whisper: "We always have our guests start dinner, but your colleagues will lose interest ten minutes in, especially if they've enjoyed the cocktail party. Which we want them to do! So . . . we try to make things as . . . straightforward as possible for our corporate customers."

"Ah." Riley supposed a meringue might flummox her colleagues. She could see Juliet continuing to study her. She glanced in a mirror on the wall, a mirror whose frame bore on every side the strange word "expectations." She wasn't sure what she had been expecting, but she did look as overwhelmed as she felt. She fluffed her hair and rubbed her eyes. It was only the miracle of being twenty-nine that kept her looking presentable. She turned away to take in the magnificent kitchen's gorgeous stone backsplashes, granite counters, and white cupboards.

A ten-year-old girl sat writing something at a table in the corner. "How's the essay coming, Faye?" Juliet called. The girl just shook her head as she labored over her homework. "Hmm . . . I wonder if there might be something in our trip to that farmer's market in Brooklyn last week? You always spot the most illuminating details." Juliet turned to Riley. "Artisanal food central. Pickles. Sourdough. Kimchi. And a craft fair in this old warehouse too. The crazy part is everyone seems to want to know about it. I've had Betsy and Faye write short pieces for the website about a Brooklyn knitting club or a cheese-making cooperative and people eat it up." She shrugged. In the corner, another girl, who looked about twelve, snapped photos of a fabulously fat baby dressed in non-seasonally-appropriate Easter clothes. Without even waiting for Riley's question, Juliet said, "We're doing an Easter-themed package across a lot of our properties in March, but that means the content gets done now. Betsy is a real pro at this. Her eye for color combinations! That pink sweater and yellow pants just *work*."

Riley pondered this woman, and how she seemed to be contemplating the skills and development of every single person she encountered. She had untold projects going on, yet Riley had never seen anyone so calm. The contrast with her own still-clenched jaw—three weeks, and her colleagues in that parlor would eject her suddenly single and friendless self from their midst—just heightened her distress.

As Juliet showed her the craft classrooms, Riley caught sight of her bracelet again. She saw more letters: *C-H-O-O-S-E*. "You emailed your photos so we could print them for your scrapbook, right?" Juliet asked.

"I . . ." Riley knew that unless her assistant had sent in photos while canceling her lunch plans with Skip, she'd have nothing.

"Ten favorite ones from your phone. That will work. How about your last vacation?"

"I . . . can't remember my last vacation."

"Or maybe pictures of someone special in your life?"

Riley imagined that Juliet meant nothing by this, but it was a punch to the gut. Neil. He was such a go-getter, Riley rued, that he'd probably already secured a new date for Saturday night. She was never going to meet the relatives he'd told her about. She was never going to make scrapbooks about *their* time together . . . "I'm sure I'll find something later . . ." she said, as her eyes watered up again.

"Oh, it's no trouble. Do you need to look to jog your memory?"

Juliet stood there and waited, her attention fully focused on her guest. She didn't seem unhappy about this moment of stillness. Indeed, she smiled at Riley as if there was nothing she would rather do than share this moment with her.

So Riley did as she was told. She pulled out her phone and tried not to look at the shots of Neil at that beer garden. She seized upon the fall photos she had just taken. They would do. "Just let me know where to send these, and I'll do that later . . ."

"We've got time now. Send them to pictures at JSP dot com and Kylie will print them up."

Riley looked up, incredulous. "Um, OK . . . I can, I just don't mean to take so much of your time while I do this and . . ."

"Oh, Riley." Juliet laughed. "I have all the time in the world."

Chapter 4

A few hours later, after a mix of work-related meetings and crafting classes, the women of MB gathered to sit at the bar on the second-floor balcony, looking out at the sea. The weather had taken a darker turn. Storm clouds rolled in thick. The waves turned choppy as the last few beach-goers, those brave souls set on visiting the seashore despite the looming October chill, packed their blankets and coolers. The mottled vines on the school's fence posts fluttered. The red leaves of the black gums and the orange of the shadbush glowed bright against the gray sky and the white lighthouse a few miles down the shore, setting off the darker colors of the pines and cedars.

All afternoon, while stuck with her colleagues, Riley had been feeling strangely claustrophobic. She was more aware than ever of the ticking clock. It was only by looking out at the water that she found relief. There, all seemed open. The wind made the balcony cool, and everyone fetched their jackets as the temperature dropped, but still, the colors, the wildness, made it a magical place.

Finally, Nadia rose to give a toast. "That was amazing. Some of you have talents I had no idea about. Jean, if the consulting thing doesn't work out, you could start a business making centerpieces. I heard Juliet say they could make you a star." Everyone laughed, Jean included, but as Riley smiled, the image from that beige conference room flashed into her mind. Soon they would be meeting again. Reviewing everything again. *Challenges.* "But I'm not surprised. MB consultants have so many talents . . ."

And so on it went. Riley couldn't focus with her job on the line. So she pulled out her phone—576 emails. She looked at one. Some question about a meeting tomorrow. Sunday? She heard Nadia say her name, but she had no idea what she'd said. So she put her phone in her pocket and smiled a little—a smile that could be appropriate for any occasion. The group laughed. It was a light laugh, a gentle laugh. Or a scolding laugh? She had no idea. She was struggling through the logistics of being at a meeting on Sunday, and getting out of the Jersey Shore. Could she fly to Atlanta for a midday meeting . . . ? She looked again. No, the meeting had happened a week before. Why was she was being copied on this email? She realized someone else had spoken to her. She nodded, distracted. A former client in London wrote about talking. He had been a royal pain. She'd race to Heathrow, only to be kept waiting for hours and strung along on work. She'd vowed not to work with him again. But if she was losing her clients, what choice did she have? She could drive to New York that night, work up a proposal with a team on Sunday, and be in London for an 8 a.m. meeting on Monday.

She was still hunting through her cluttered calendar when she noticed, a minute later, that she and the bartender were the only people left on the balcony. The sun set behind the school, sinking beneath the roofs of the other Victorian houses, the cedars and persimmons. The bartender packed up his bottles. "They went inside to cook dinner. Are you going? Or trying to get out of it?" He laughed. "I get a straggler or two up here every event. People who cook for their families and don't get the appeal of paying to do it."

"No, I was looking forward to that part, I guess I just . . ."

"I can make you something strong enough to take you through the next hour if you want to stay here and enjoy the view in peace."

"No, no, I . . ." Riley put her phone back in her pocket, flustered. Should she go to London?

Juliet popped her head out the door. "Well, there you are! Kevin wondered where his apprentice had gone. Were you off in your own little world?"

"Yes," Riley said. "But it wasn't a great place to be."

Juliet didn't laugh this off like Riley thought she would. "Why wouldn't it be a good place? What possibilities are you imagining?"

Riley shook her head. She couldn't talk about it now, though something about the woman made her want to. She sensed that energy again, crackling over the balcony. Juliet's eyes were gentle. She looked like she had time for anything you might tell her.

"Anyway, you can't imagine how happy Kevin was to learn at least one person wasn't going to drift back to the bar after listening to him for thirty seconds." Riley took one last look at the darkening ocean. The choppy water splashed high against a motorboat rumbling in for the night. She followed Juliet downstairs to the kitchen, where her colleagues were, as promised, all gripping their glasses and watching other people do the work.

But Riley, also as promised, was going all in until she achieved competence. Kevin, whom Juliet introduced as an import from Kyoto, handed Riley the nicest knife she'd ever held. The handle felt smooth and substantial in her grasp. He showed her how to slice, to hold the onion with one palm and rock the knife with the other. Her first cuts were rough, producing cubes the size of dice. They'd suffice for her college braises, but not for now. Kevin pushed those cubes to the side. Her second attempt was better; the third onion was, after furious chopping, reduced to pieces as small as baby teeth. Kevin applauded. Riley grabbed a fourth onion and leaned into this one. The world around her, the colleagues who were going to fire her, her swirling thoughts of Neil sharing a dessert by candlelight with someone else, all disappeared. She threw herself into her chopping. Her arm ached. She didn't care. Another onion. Another. Kevin called Juliet over to photograph these onions, compared to the "before" pile from her first attempt.

"Wow, Riley," Juliet said in appreciation. "You know how to work, don't you?"

"That's what I do," Riley said. She looked up. Her colleagues stared at her. *Yes,* she thought. *That's what I do. No matter what it requires of me, I roll up my sleeves and I* work. The women of MB resumed their conversations. The duck and the Brussels sprouts went into the oven first as two staff members poured soup into bowls. Bob ushered the women to their seats. Riley knew she should join everyone, but with Juliet standing there, watching her, she couldn't pull herself away. Finally, tentatively: "How do *you* decide what to do?"

Juliet pondered this. "You mean like which projects to do? What to do in any moment? What to do with my life?" She grabbed a glass of sparkling wine off Harold's tray and handed it to Riley.

"Any of that. All of that. You seem calm despite everything you have going on."

Juliet nodded. "I think a lot about how I spend my time," she said. "Twenty-four hours in a day. One hundred and sixty-eight hours in a week. It is a lot of time from the perspective of fitting in what matters to me, but it is ultimately a precious resource too. I cannot do everything, so I do what I find most meaningful and enjoyable to myself and the people I care about."

"You make it sound simple."

"It is."

"But I have six hundred and fifty-seven unread messages

in my inbox from people who need me. How would I only do what I wanted?"

"I believe you used the word 'simple,' not easy."

Riley sighed. "I shouldn't be here. I have so much I need to do. If I don't land new clients in the next three weeks they're going to fire me. They seem nice, but MB is brutal about stuff like that."

"Oh, Riley." Juliet smiled. "Perhaps you could see other possibilities?" She raised her glass and met Riley's eyes. That same strange sense of knowing. What could Juliet see? Riley nodded and took her seat, returning, of course, to her ghastly inbox even before the soup course ended. Nadia proposed another toast—826 unread messages. How could this jumble of expectations be swelling so quickly? One from Skip. *Can you talk tomorrow for a few minutes? The donor wants to move our meeting to a Sunday afternoon coffee since something came up for Monday. Riley, can you please respond?* She meant to. But she had nothing. No ideas. Her brain felt strained.

It was as if Nadia could see this mental clutter. "Here's to our brilliance!" she said, a few drinks in. "Here's to MB, where the insights come so fast we can't catch them all." Everyone raised their glasses. Riley could barely taste her duck, could barely talk to her tablemates. What would she do if she didn't make it at MB? What would she tell her parents, who bragged about her success to their neighbors? She had, in idle moments, seen herself leading these toasts someday, just like she had daydreamed about Neil. She wanted to rise as high as she could at MB. She wanted to seek out projects and clients that fascinated her. When she was being interviewed for her job, years before, she remembered talking about bringing MB's capacity to broader social issues—to the talent development, perhaps, of girls like her from the world's less-mined quarters. She wanted time to think about such things. She wanted to have enough energy to enjoy the people she loved. She glanced for the first time at the table centerpieces. Little clocks. And this phrase, woven onto the mats under them: *Time is finite.* What was with this place? The hours, with her inbox, were spinning out of her control.

She grew dizzy, but no one seemed to notice. A woman from the Washington, DC, office prattled on about a recent trip to Napa. The meringue emerged, and was consumed, and the women drifted toward that upholstered parlor. Riley lingered at her table. She kept staring at the clock. She felt Juliet watching her from the doorway. She could not face more hours feigning interest. She wasn't sure about everyone else's holidays in wine country, but she didn't have space amid her finite time for such things. Maybe her colleagues were luckier. Maybe they knew people she didn't. Maybe—born into privilege, funneled into Ivy League degrees, feeling fully entitled to all good things that came to them—they didn't know what it was like to be constantly proving yourself.

In any case, as Juliet said, Riley knew how to work. She was *not* going to be outworked.

So she slipped out of the room. She climbed the narrow stairs to her hallway. She recognized her room at once from the giant starfish on the door. She turned the knob and walked in. Her duffel bag sat on the luggage stand. Bob had done what he could, but her bag looked as beat up as she felt. Riley ran the numbers. That little leather carry-on, chosen over a roll-aboard because it would never need to be gate-checked, and thus she could always be first in the taxi line, had spent the equivalent of four months out of the last four years stuffed into overhead compartments. None of it had led to anything but proving herself below average.

She picked up her phone again—1,074 unread messages. The panic rose. This could not be possible. It was Saturday. What was going on? Was she hallucinating? She could barely breathe. She looked at one randomly. Another. Was she going to London? Or there was that grocery store chain headquartered in Atlanta. She could fly there Monday and walk the halls. She glanced out the window. Storm clouds gathered in the night sky. Far away, she heard a crack of thunder. The sounds downstairs grew fainter. People walked, chatting, down the hall. She heard her own name. A laugh. She listened closer. "Did you see she didn't even get her head out of her phone when Nadia mentioned her in that toast?" Another laugh.

Doors opened. Then all was silent.

Riley listened to the silence for a few minutes. She looked down—1,136 unread messages. The number rose like seconds on a stop watch. She buried her head in her hands.

Then, after a long time, she heard a knock. "Riley?" said Juliet. "It's me."

Chapter 5

Riley put down her phone. She paused. What should she do? It wasn't every day that a celebrity took an inexplicable interest in one's life. It would be rude not to open the door and invite her in. She supposed she could always tell Juliet she was too busy to talk, though "busy" was clearly relative. The rational part of her brain knew it was improbable that she had more on her plate than a single mother raising two children and running a sprawling business. And the truth was, other parts of her brain wanted to talk.

Opening the door would itself be a decision. It would be a decision not to spend the next few minutes recruiting a team to meet on Sunday and analyze the needs of the London or Atlanta clients. She felt paralyzed. The clock was ticking. Twenty days. She couldn't just not deal with all this.

Yet there was the knock again. Calmly persistent. Just like Juliet.

"Riley!" she called. "Riley, my dear, I'm pretty sure you're in there." Her light was on; she couldn't pretend to be asleep. She sighed and opened the door.

Juliet stood there, covered from head to toe in rain gear. She held a second raincoat in her arms.

"Hey," Riley said, confused. She had somewhat assumed there would be another mug of mulled wine involved in this visitation. "Are you going somewhere?"

"Yes," she said. "*We* are going somewhere. I think we have an hour before the rain really starts. The storm is coming in. Have you seen the beach in a storm?"

"I'm not sure I . . ."

"I love wild nights like this. Nights like this are full of possibilities."

"Or emails," said Riley. "I've got over a thousand unread

messages. Probably up to twelve hundred now that I've looked away for a minute."

"Or twelve thousand!" Juliet said. "I think I have twenty-four thousand unread emails in my inbox. Here's the funny thing: They'll still be there later." She held out the second raincoat. "Come walk with me."

"We're going out in the storm?"

"I have something I want to show you. I have something you need to see." Juliet looked Riley straight in the eyes. She smiled. There was no escaping that gaze. Riley shoved her phone in her pocket, but Juliet motioned to her charger on the desk. "Leave it—I wouldn't want it to get wet if I'm wrong on the rain."

Reluctantly, Riley put it down. She slid into the coat. She felt oddly swaddled in it, like everything extraneous was being muffled out.

The halls of Juliet's school were quiet. A few conversations drifted out of a few doors, but for the most part the consultants were all working alone. Juliet and Riley walked down the stairs and passed Harold and Bob cleaning up from the evening. Harold pulled two plates at a time out of the dishwasher, stacking them in the cupboard. Bob set the table for breakfast. Juliet whispered something to them. They looked at Riley in her borrowed raincoat and nodded knowingly. Riley had a feeling that this was not the first time Juliet had taken a customer out on a stormy night. Bob gave her a salute.

"Ready?" Juliet opened the door with the shellacked wreath. The night guard glanced up from the guardhouse, but she motioned him to stay put. He nodded. It was late enough. The beach was deserted. She didn't have her highly recognized children with her. She could go unaccompanied.

As they stepped outside, the blustery wind took Riley's breath away. From the porch she could see the dark choppy water reflecting a light from the pier. Waves broke against the pier's wooden posts. Angry plumes of spray hissed into the air. Two people on the boardwalk wrapped their coats tighter and hurried off.

"Come on!" Juliet called. Now she was laughing as a flash of lightning blazed on the horizon. Thirty seconds later, a rumble like a train growled through the hunkered-down town. The storm was still a few miles off. "We have time! We have all the time in the world."

It was the second time she had said that phrase to Riley. She pulled her down the steps, over the road, and up the path to the boardwalk. The wind picked up the closer they came to the beach. Up on the boardwalk it seemed to roar around them. Another flash of lightning illuminated the lighthouse in the distance and made Juliet's green eyes glow. The beach grass bent back. Sand scratched past them. Juliet took Riley's arm to steady her.

It seemed improbable that one could hear anything in that din, yet when Juliet leaned close, her voice was oddly clear. She spoke low. Somehow Riley's ears could absorb it. They walked forward, past the shuttered beach tag hut, and out to the fishing dock. The wild night seemed to pull her into something different, something strange. Riley had a sudden thought. She really *shouldn't* be able to hear Juliet this well. Something odd was going on. On the horizon, the sky brightened with an otherworldly, orangish gleam.

Juliet smiled. It was a bewitching sort of grin. "Despite your achievements with the onions, I couldn't help but see how sad you seemed at dinner."

"Well, you know. I just lost my biggest client. Counting down the days until you're fired puts a damper on your mood."

"Would MB really wish to part with you?"

"You'd be surprised. According to my evaluator, I have to show progress in the next thirty days, or I will be rated the dreaded 'Resignation Suggested.'"

" 'Resignation Suggested' is the dumbest euphemism I have ever heard," Juliet said.

"You just fire people?"

She stopped and thought. "I haven't had to. I put a lot of effort into hiring people—and once people are in, I know they're good. Even if they have slow patches, I know it's usually something we can redirect. I spend a lot of time thinking about that: how I can choose to direct their precious time wisely." Riley thought back to Jean's critique of her unfocused and over-worked teams. "And doing whatever I can to keep them."

"Like letting an employee's baby come to the office?"

"Did that surprise you?" Juliet looked off in the distance. "I mean, my kids are with me all the time, and she did come in on a Saturday to help with the retreat." She paused. "But the truth is, it's this: I keep my eye on what is most important to me. Keeping Kylie is right up there with keeping my own children. I know those twenty-four thousand unread emails in my inbox aren't important because she's told me they aren't."

Riley pondered this. She had an assistant. But she had never thought about delegating that.

"So you're worried about your job? Is that all?"

"All? I've always wanted to work for MB. They hire five hundred people out of thirty thousand who apply every year.

All people who went to Princeton, Harvard . . . not Indiana like me. No one from where I grew up had any clue about places like MB . . ." She stopped. "But no, not all. My boyfriend called when I was on the way here and said it was over."

"Oh, Riley, I'm sorry. I'm sorry it happened by phone too."

Riley sighed. "That was my fault. My best friend chewed me out about that and I'll own it. He'd been trying to meet in person for the past three weeks, and I kept having to travel and crash on these proposals and cancel our plans."

"I see."

"And Skip—that's my best friend—is furious at me because I was supposed to help her brainstorm ideas for her nonprofit. She's meeting with a potential donor tomorrow. Something original to do with middle school girls. Do you have ideas? Because I'm so overwhelmed by everything coming at me, everything people want me to do, that I'm just stuck."

"Maybe," said Juliet. "Sometimes I have ideas. People think I specialize in the domestic arts. But really, I work in possibilities."

"What sort of possibilities?"

"That," she said, "is precisely what I want to show you."

Chapter 6

They stood on the dock. Lightning flashed over the dark water, searing holes in the sky bright enough to be day. "Look closely," Juliet said at the reddening horizon. She waved her arm—like a magician waving a wand. "Look at the clouds just over the water. I see you. Do you see you?"

Riley could not describe what had happened. But something had changed with that wave. As she peered into those whirling clouds, she *did* see herself. She supposed she might have been dreaming. Her constant exhaustion meant she fell asleep randomly, but this vision felt more lucid than those nightly torments of missed planes.

Somewhere off in this cloudscape, she was older, she could see that. At least twenty-five years older, perhaps in her mid-fifties. She looked even more tired than she felt now. She sat at the kitchen table of a nondescript if luxurious house, a builder model with nothing on the walls to distinguish it. A girl, about ten years old, sat across from her. "Is that my . . . daughter?" Riley asked.

"No—a neighbor's child," Juliet said. "She has a question for you."

The little girl leaned in. "*I'm supposed to interview a neighbor for a Girl Scout badge,*" she said. "My mom said she thought you seemed lonely so I came over here."

The real Riley flinched. Juliet could see this all too. "Kids," she said. "They say . . . insightful things."

"Maybe." Riley in the vision sighed. "I've got a few minutes. What do you want to hear about?"

"Tell me about your first job," the girl said.

"Well, I worked as a waitress in college, and in this casino for a summer, but my first real *real* job after business school was at a consulting firm, MB & Company. You've probably never heard of it but . . ." The vision swirled to Riley, alarmingly close to her current age, sitting in a beige conference room. She recognized a voice. Jean. She was reading from a typed page with a very legalistic voice. Words in these cases had to be chosen in advance, vetted by the proper departments. It could wind up in court, and MB strove to ensure that no court case had a chance of going anywhere because of procedural sloppiness. *"Resignation Suggested."* Riley's eyes grew wide. In the vision, she sat silent. Jean filled the silence. *"I know I'm not supposed to say anything other than what's on this paper, but let's be real human beings, OK? You're burned out, Riley. It's going to be a blessing for you. I don't think you're happy here. It's OK. Not everyone does well with the pressure. But you get three months of paid search time. Please take your time and figure out what you really want to do."*

"I have a job offer already," Riley in the vision snapped. She did. The vision swirled forward, to Riley on more planes, more quiet offices after everyone else had gone home, and then a few years later, another conference room. Another voice. *"It's not that you're not hardworking . . ."* Riley's voice: "I never took a vacation the entire time I've been here. I've been all in for this . . ." The other voice: *"Of course. But you know our industry is in trouble. We need someone with big ideas to lead this section.*

And honestly, the feedback we got is that when other employees talk to you, they just get stressed out." The scene whirled out, then a third conference room appeared. Riley and another evaluator were having the exact same conversation. A fourth . . .

The little girl wrote some things down in her notebook. "Do you have children?"

Riley in the vision laughed. "Oh no—I can't even keep houseplants alive. I'm always so busy, traveling, you know . . . right?" The little girl looked mystified. "I was married for a while," Riley volunteered. "I don't know why I'm telling you this."

"Why is she telling her this?" the real Riley said, plaintively.

"Shh . . ." Juliet said. "She hasn't talked with anyone in a while. She wants to talk. Just let her."

"But, you know, these things don't always last." Riley at the kitchen table shrugged. "I guess we just grew apart, and there wasn't anything keeping us together."

"Oh." The little girl frowned. Riley in the vision got up to get her a snack. She searched through her pantry, but saw nothing of interest.

"Sorry," she said. "I've got some crackers, maybe? These chips seem stale. I guess I've been too busy to get to the grocery store lately. I used to like to cook but . . . I just eat a lot of take-out. Work takes all my time and I'm too busy to cook . . ."

"I don't think you told me about your job right now?" the girl asked.

"Oh, I'm . . ." Riley paused. "It's hard to describe what I'm doing. Strategy stuff. It's not that exciting. I mean, it's work. It pays the bills. It's not supposed to be fun. That's why they call it work!"

"I cannot *believe* those words came out of my mouth," current Riley groused. She would have hated anyone who said such a thing to her, and here she was, bellowing it out as the truth. What was this? What was this miserable woman doing to this girl?

"I just have one more question. I know you're busy," the little girl said, leaning forward. This one was going in for the kill. "Of all the things you've done in your life, what are you *most* proud of?"

Even in the whirling storm, there was silence. The silence lasted. Future Riley sat at that table with her coffee, staring into it. "To be honest, I just don't know," she said. "I mean, there must be something but . . . *I don't know.*"

With that, the vision whisked off, somewhere into the dark sky. Riley saw nothing but the waves.

It took her a minute to realize she was still gripping Juliet's hand. "What was that?" she said. Her voice was more angry than sad. "What the hell was that?"

"A possibility." Juliet smiled slightly. "Just one possibility. I take it you don't like what you saw?"

"It was bleak—it was . . ."

"Not how you picture your future? It wasn't terrible. You're employed. It looks like an expensive house. You have at least one nice neighbor."

"Yes, I suppose . . ."

"But Riley Jenkins has never fathomed a future where she was living on the street. It's something *else* that's bothering you."

"Yes," Riley said, now more sure. "It's the lack of impact. It's that she's working so hard, but slipping through life . . ."

"She always has so much to do and yet nothing that matters gets done. Is that it?"

"My days feel like that now," Riley said, quiet. "There is so much I could do. There is so much that I want to do. I'm just always so busy and . . ."

"Our actions determine our courses. How we live our hours is how we live our lives." Juliet paused. "Could how you live your hours lead to a place where you can't even say what you're proud of? As I talk to you, I see someone who everyone knows has such potential."

"But there is a moment when potential must become what you're actually doing, or else I'm sitting in that miserable kitchen having done nothing with my life. And so . . ."

Juliet tapped her bracelet. "Would you like to see something else? Because, Riley, there is another possibility too."

Chapter 7

They turned back toward the churning clouds. Riley took Juliet's outstretched hand. She felt that now-familiar crackle. Another flash of lightning split the sky. An image slowly pulled itself together out of the pieces. Skip. Her long blond hair was short now. It was a middle-aged woman's cut, and she wore a no-nonsense business suit instead of the jeans and sweaters Skip usually sported, but it was definitely Skip. She was earnest as always. She stood behind a podium on a stage with huge banners behind her. Riley could not make out what they said, but the atmosphere was festive. People laughed, clapped. Skip herself was beaming.

"*Ladies and gentlemen, I am thrilled to be here tonight.* Oh yes, I know I always say that. And I always love to celebrate the work we do, but tonight is special. I'm particularly thrilled to spend time with my great friend Riley . . ."

The scene swirled over to future Riley, sitting in a chair toward the front of a huge ballroom. She looked relaxed. Happy. In every way she looked healthier than the woman in the kitchen in that first possibility.

"You all know Riley as the inspirational CEO of MB & Company . . ."

"The *what*?" Riley in real life was flabbergasted.

"Shush . . ." Juliet said. "Just hear her out."

"Consultants don't like to talk about the work they do for their clients, but we can talk about a few things. Right, Riley? Can I do that?" Skip in the vision smiled at her friend. "Riley announced when she took over five years ago that she would put real capacity into a few subversive little ventures. She said, look, we already hire the smartest people in the world. Why can't we use them to *change* the world?" Skip paced the stage. "So she formed a small business advisory service and enrolled mostly female entrepreneurs from all over the globe in training similar to what MB consultants get. The goal was to help them grow their businesses to more than $1 million in revenue. A full three-quarters of the first cohort hit that mark."

The room burst into applause. "But of course, you shouldn't think this is altruism *at all*. She wants these small businesses to become big enough to be MB clients. Right, Riley?"

There in the front row, Riley laughed. "Some already are!" Riley heard her own voice. It was positively merry.

"Then there's the international education work. She formed a squad of consultants to go into the dozen countries with the lowest rates of school enrollment for girls, and they worked to implement as many best practices as possible. In five years, the attendance rate has risen 5 percent in those dozen countries. This is literally thousands of young women's lives. That sounds more altruistic to me, but maybe not. If I know Riley, she's probably scheming to have some of those women wind up as MB clients or consultants too." The audience laughed.

"And of course there's the work she's done for *us*. You all— all our donors—know that we are managed as well as any for-profit company. We get gold stars on all our audits. We do a lot with our dollars. You know that 92 percent of the girls who've gone through our programs go to college. Some of you have been with us for a while, and twenty years ago when our first girls were going to college we were shouting our 92 percent figure from the rooftops. But it was Riley who challenged us to do more. She said, 'Listen, Skip. There are a lot of colleges. Anyone can get people enrolled. The challenge is whether you can get them *through*.' Thanks to Riley's tracking systems, and the interventions she helped us build, we know that 83 percent of our girls who start college finish in six years. This is a lot of amazing young women. And . . ." The audience waited for it. *"Riley would know because she keeps recruiting them!"*

Skip threw up her hands. "It all helps MB somehow but it does a lot of good in the meantime so I won't begrudge her that. And so I am excited to honor my great friend Riley with this lifetime achievement award for all the impact she's had."

Riley watched this vision of herself standing up to get her award. "Is that really possible?" she asked Juliet. "I'm the CEO of MB?"

"Well, why not?" Juliet asked. "Someone has to be. More likely someone who works there than someone who doesn't. I see possibilities. Isn't that a possibility?"

"I suppose, it's just . . . well . . . there haven't been any women at the top of MB before. We had to go pretty far down the ranks—like to me—to get enough women to fill your rooms. I think everyone assumes you can't raise a family and do this and . . ." She paused. "I know one of these visions is of my professional success, and the other is not, but I sort of assumed the 'not' would be because I needed to scale back when I had kids . . ."

"A false choice," said Juliet. "Absolutely a false choice. The same mind-set that creates space for world-changing ideas creates space for real relationships. The mind-set that chokes off such ideas and their execution chokes off the choice to go all in on all forms of meaning." Juliet waited while Riley pondered this. Then she smiled. "Look closer."

Riley squinted into the clouds above the water. She tried to see what details she was missing.

Juliet decided to help her imagination along. "I see a man sitting at your table." Her voice took on a slightly conspiratorial tone as she narrated this. "A tall man. Very blond hair. Must be Scandinavian. I'd guess Danish. Nice-looking fellow, Riley. Looks like he's very athletic! Maybe a cyclist?"

Riley searched for the image Juliet described, but it was too dark to see this very specific man. "I guess I'll have to trust you on that one."

"Quite the catch. And who are these fine young men at your table, watching their mother with such pride? Three teenage boys whom you've managed to get into suits and who are behaving themselves at a fundraising dinner. Good for you. You've raised them well. Definitely a wise choice of how to spend your time."

Riley on the beach watched Riley in that banquet hall walk onstage to accept her award. Riley twenty-five years hence embraced Skip, and the two women beamed at each other with affection born of a three-decade friendship that nurtured not only them, but everyone who came into their orbit.

"OK," said Riley. "I find this image improbable—not only that someone rated 'below average' could ascend to glory but that the men who run MB magically lost all bias in the CEO selection process . . ."

"*Not* magic." Juliet turned toward the shore. "My guess is that someone with great ideas got involved in the hiring process to make sure that new hires had new mind-sets, and got involved in the promotion process to make sure it was done fairly. By the time MB's partners elected their CEO twenty years from now, people had different ideas of what leaders looked like. And they knew a leader who had already shown concern for making the most of all of their talents . . ."

Riley shook her head. "OK, I believe you that it is a possibility. Just like the other depressing possibility." She scanned the sky once more. "So what is the difference between these futures? Something I need to do? Ebenezer Scrooge wakes up and realizes it's not too late to choose his future."

Juliet laughed. "For that, I need to tell you a different story."

"A third possibility? A Christmas Past?"

"In a way," she said. "It's a story about me."

Chapter 8

The two women walked back down the pier, and onto the boardwalk. The night grew more blustery. Juliet turned south toward the lighthouse. Riley struggled to keep up. "You're not the only one to wonder about improbable-seeming possibilities," Juliet said as they passed her school. The shrubbery surrounding the front yard bent in the wind, the undersides of leaves glimmering pale in the lamplight. A few leaves fluttered out into the sky. The guard peeked out of his hut to check on them. Juliet waved, but they kept walking. "Eight years ago I was living in western Pennsylvania—a small town you have never heard of—with the girls and my ex-husband."

"I think Wikipedia said something about that . . ." Riley stopped. Admitting her internet research was perhaps *amateurish,* as Elsa might have put it.

But Juliet didn't seem to care. "We were young. A mistake, perhaps. It gave me my girls."

"So there's that. But he didn't last?"

She shrugged. "Too much responsibility. We fought all the time, and then—I'd been waitressing a few hours at night and on weekends when he could be home—I came home one night and he *wasn't* home. Two little girls, sitting in front of the TV in our apartment, all alone, waiting for me." Juliet shuddered at the memory.

Riley wasn't sure what to say, but it seemed Juliet didn't want her to say anything. So she stayed silent.

"Anyway, there were court appearances and a lawyer I couldn't afford, but that all happened later. At the time, I think I stayed there shaking and crying in bed for a day. Then Faye threw up, so I had to get out of bed to do laundry. When I hauled the three of us to the laundry room, I found a woman there who had also been crying. I figured I may as well talk to her. It turned out she was upset because her mom could no longer watch her kids during the day while she was working. I needed someone at night. We decided to trade shifts."

"Quite the stroke of luck," Riley said.

"It bought me time. It also gave me my best craft ideas. Entertaining four small children all day is no joke." She got quiet for a minute. "But anyway, we survived. And as I settled into that life, I started having all these ideas for the restaurant where I was working. New menu items. Changes in decor. My manager had no interest, so I told my ideas to anyone else who would listen. The only person who cared was one patron who started coming there with friends every Thursday."

"Yes?"

"He owned a small inn outside town. I had heard of the place. It was more luxurious than anything else in the area. He listened to my ideas for six months and then he asked if I was looking for a job. His hotel manager had quit and he needed someone. So the girls and I moved out to the caretaker's cottage. Much nicer digs. He was OK with me working while they were at preschool, or while they played in the yard. They often wanted to help me. That's where they learned how to decorate, to plan menus . . ." She looked back toward the school. "We started getting written up in travel magazines. A little gem in western Pennsylvania. I was so grateful."

"And?"

"And then my happiness became misery, because I stopped worrying we were going to starve. I started thinking about possibilities," she said. "My *own* business. My own empire of the domestic arts. My own properties. A retreat center housed in an old hotel by the ocean, which I saw advertised for sale in the *Wall Street Journal*. I got so mad at myself for thinking of these things."

"Because?"

"Because I didn't have the time! I was too busy."

"You *were* busy."

"Yes! I had two young daughters. I was a single mother, newly escaped from penury. And there was always something else to do for the inn. I could come up with a package I could pitch the magazines. Fall foliage. The best gardens of western Pennsylvania. I redid every room in that inn with a different theme. So there were a million contractors, and all the emails about meetings with them, and the budgets, and any time that wasn't consumed by that was spent figuring out stuff with the girls."

"Feeling like you're constantly behind . . ."

"Wanting to think about my business, but I'd get to the end of the day and there wouldn't be any time left over."

"But here we are." Riley looked at Juliet. "So, what happened?"

"I was complaining about my lack of time to one of our housekeepers. She had been there forever. She never said much, which is probably why I was complaining to her. I'd babble and she'd keep wiping down the counters. But one night, she stopped me. I remember, it was a rainy, stormy night like this one. The girls were watching a movie in the lounge while I was theoretically cleaning out my inbox. She looked up from wiping down the counters, and she said, 'You have been talking about this business you want to start for the last forty-five minutes. And you talked about it Tuesday night for thirty.'"

"She'd been keeping track?"

"I guess. Who knows? But I heard the question she was asking within that number: What else could I have done with that time I spent complaining about my lack of time?"

"Start writing a business plan?"

"Maybe. But as I was sputtering about that, she looked me in the eye and told me that if someone offered to give me half a million dollars to start my business on condition of my producing a viable business plan, I would probably find the time to cough it up. I protested that no half million was on offer, and she told me it never would be if I didn't get started. I could pretend someone was offering the cash. That would make it a top priority for me. And then she said this. I will remember these words forever."

"Yes?"

"'I don't have time' means 'It's not a priority.' We always have time for what matters to us." Juliet paused. "I wrote that down. I made myself write that phrase over and over. *We always have time for what matters to us.*"

"But is that true?"

"You don't think so?"

"You had a million things going on. I have a million things going on. OK, probably less than you with two small children, so you had two million things going on. We can't just *not* do the things other people are expecting us to do."

"Why not?"

It was a good question. Riley thought about it. "In my case, because I work for a company. They pay me a lot. More than a small-town Indiana girl like me ever had any hope to expect. And so I need to deliver on what is expected of me."

"I agree that we need to deliver results. I saw tonight that you are willing to roll up your sleeves when presented with a challenge. But are you absolutely clear on what is expected of you?"

"What do you mean? I need to do what my clients and colleagues tell me and . . ."

"Maybe. It is often easier to meet the expectations that are flashing right in front of us instead of the expectations that are more important, but more nebulous. And here's the thing: There can be infinite expectations. Even if you never slept, you could not meet all the expectations of your employer, your colleagues, your clients, your friends, your family, yourself. You cannot do everything; the choice to meet one expectation is always a choice not to meet another." Juliet paused. "The difficult truth in this is that sometimes you need to disappoint someone's obvious expectation in order to eventually meet bigger ones."

Riley pondered this. "Don't answer the email immediately so you have space to think about the bigger problem? Don't agree to a meeting just because you're available if it's not the best use of anyone's time?"

"Perhaps. And sometimes, when we are honest with ourselves, some expectations are self-imposed. Or maybe we have blind spots. As the housekeeper noted, I'd found time to complain about all that I didn't have time to do." She thought back. "I remember standing there writing down these words from the counter-wiping oracle when she pointed out something else.

'*Remember when the creek rose after that storm? Remember when it flooded the basement?*' We'd had this horrible wet spell a few months before. I'd spent hours getting the rugs replaced. 'Where did that time come from?' she asked me. 'You didn't make more time. And yet if the basement hadn't flooded, you would have claimed you were busy that week too, because the time would have been filled with something else. When the basement flooded, you chucked that something else because it didn't matter.' And here's where she got me. She said this: '*You could have chosen to chuck it without the basement flooding. You can figure out what's important to you and treat it like a flooded basement.*'"

"In other words, you decide it is important enough to get to it *now*."

"I thought there was something to what she said. And so that night, as Betsy and Faye were watching *Finding Nemo,* I tried this mental experiment. I don't know if it is true that I have time for what matters to me. *But what if I behaved as if it were true?*"

"If you just told yourself you had all the time in the world?"

"That phrase! You've been listening. And why not? I have as much time as anyone else. Rushing just made me feel rushed. Telling myself I had no time made me feel like I had no time.

When I told myself I had time for what mattered, something *did* change. I saw that I could forget the existential angst of my predicament and simply sit down at my computer for the next hour and write. So I did. The next night I did the same. I had a contractor cancel the next day, and instead of jumping back on email, I spent time analyzing the services I could provide, and how I would build up my brand."

"And eventually you made the leap?"

"I started a few things on the side. My blog. I tried doing webinars. I had the girls film my first videos. They used a tripod but still. I cannot believe we got traffic. I got emails about sponsorships and ad possibilities. I mean, a lot of queries. It was like this message from the universe. Eventually I had to talk to the inn's owner."

"Since it was taking too much time?"

"The more immediate reason was that I needed permission to take photos of projects I'd done at the inn. But, funny enough, the day before I planned to talk with him, I heard from a producer at the *Today* show who wondered if I had video of me cooking. They thought I could fill in for a segment while their usual guy was on vacation. I didn't have anything professional. What was I going to do? And then I met with the inn's owner, and he wanted to learn more."

"And you had a business plan."

"I did. He looked it over and a few hours later he said, '*Look*, this is good stuff. You are going to be big, and I want to invest in this company. I have friends who want to invest in this. Can we?' I mentioned they could start by hiring a camera man who wasn't six years old."

"So the hypothetical scenario the housekeeper proposed came to be."

"Something not far from it, once I chose to spend my time in ways that helped bring that vision about. Of course, running a business, there are always even more things I could be doing. More emails. More people who want to meet. More projects. The choices are *hard*."

"Yes," Riley said. "The expectations are infinite . . ."

"But it is still the same as she told me. I have to see the vision of the life I want. I have to ask of every minute, of every decision, every obligation I choose to take on: Is this bringing me closer to that vision? Or am I doing it just because it's there? After a while, I formulated my own version of her insight. I inscribed it everywhere:

Expectations are infinite.

Time is finite.

You are always choosing.

Choose well.

"I look at that statement when I wake up. I look at it when I go to bed. It is all over the school. Have you seen it?"

Riley thought back to the phrases on the clocks, the mirror, the door. "I saw snippets . . ."

"Now you know to look. And when you know to look, you will see."

She held up her bracelet, and as the lighthouse beam pulsed in the distance, Riley could see the words etched on it: *Choose well.*

"I look at it when I decide to have a difficult conversation with an employee rather than bury myself in my inbox. I think about it when I set my quarterly goals each year, when I plan my weeks, thinking through my business priorities, my family goals, and what I need to do to be a whole person myself. Expectations are infinite. I could fill every minute. We all could. Therefore, the only way to do anything big in life is to choose which expectations—including my own expectations—are worthy of this ultimately limited resource."

Chapter 9

Juliet and Riley stood there, staring at each other. Neither said a word. Then, after what seemed like hours, a peal of thunder shook them out of their silence. The storm was almost upon them. Juliet spun around and set them hustling, even more briskly than before, toward the school. Riley raced to keep up. A few raindrops fell on her face. She pulled the coat tighter. "I think we'd better spend the next few minutes choosing to run!" Juliet yelled.

They dashed down the boardwalk. The rain fell harder. It accelerated from drops to sheets. Soon it was pelting so hard that they could barely see. They raced faster, splashing, along the boardwalk, blown by the gale, across the road, through the front yard of the school, where the guard was standing in the hut with his flashlight, watching for them. He nodded, relieved. He shook his head as they ran, soaked, up to the porch.

The rain blew nearly sideways. As Juliet yanked open the door with the leaf wreath, it blew them inside. "Are you OK?" Juliet said as they stood there, dripping, on the rug.

Bob—who looked more worried than usual—ran up with towels. Riley dried off her soaked hair. Any clothes that had been inside the raincoat were dry, though the bottom of her jeans were wet completely through. She looked around to hand Bob the towel and realized he had reappeared with cups of hot tea.

"Warm up!" he said. "She is actually crazy," he told Riley. "Did you know that? I should have warned you."

Juliet laughed. "Maybe crazy," she said. "Just a twist from your average corporate retreat. But I did get her back safely. And we were only gone forty minutes. A bit less than that."

Riley felt in her pocket for her phone, then remembered it was back in her room. She looked around and spotted an ornate grandfather clock in the corner. Now that she knew to look, she saw the words clearly. On the chimes themselves. *Time is finite.*

Juliet was right. Thirty-eight minutes. Had it only been that long? She felt like it had been hours. Her mind spun. She took her tea.

"Well, thank you," she told Juliet. "I appreciate your . . . showing me everything."

"Of course," she said. "Anytime. I have . . ."

"All the time in the world?"

"Certainly." She tapped her bracelet. "I love seeing possibilities."

Riley nodded and took her tea up to the starfish room. She shut the door behind her, changed from her wet jeans into sweatpants, and sat on her bed. She stared at the little balcony with its few pots of shrubbery well hidden from the rain. She looked at the art on the wall, all pictures of starfish. Big. Small. Sure enough, etched somewhere in each picture were those words:

Expectations are infinite. Time is finite. You are always choosing. Choose well.

What was she to make of this? She wanted to talk to someone, but Neil had removed himself from her chaos. Skip too, at least until Riley redeemed herself. She pictured Juliet deciding, in that little inn in western Pennsylvania, that she wanted bigger things in life. She pictured her choosing how to spend her minutes in order to bring this life to fruition. Then she pondered these visions of her own future. She felt herself in that triumphant ballroom. And she felt herself in that lonely kitchen. These two images tangled up with each other, the colors and words blurring into one struggle.

It was too much. Riley knew what felt comforting when she didn't know what to do. She picked up her phone and began hacking away at the 1,247 unread messages stacked up—all these little birds in the nest, waiting for their worms. A meeting in Geneva in December that somebody else would be attending. A reminder about the correct archiving procedure for slide decks. Someone's question about the lack of coffee creamer in the office fridge, with a follow-up note confessing that it was there, he just hadn't seen it. The reading, the deleting, the forwarding to someone with an FYI. It was so reassuring. So satisfying to see that number go down—1,225 . . . 1,214 . . . 1,203.

Then, all of a sudden, the room lit up, bright as day. Thunder rattled the roof. Riley heard another crack. The lamp flickered. The alarm clock on the bedside table blinked. All the little whirring noises composing the background music of modern life went silent. The power had gone out. The room was pitch-black. But as Riley felt her way toward her bag, intending to dig out her little travel flashlight, she saw something glowing outside.

"Oh!" She caught her breath. The black gum tree near her window was actually smoldering. Flames crackled from the drier parts hidden by the leaves of another tree. The lightning—had it hit it? A gust of wind blew a handful of the burning leaves off into the air . . .

. . . and right onto Riley's balcony.

She watched the shrubbery start to burn. Shielded by the roof, the plants must have been bone-dry. The flames raced up the stalks. She fumbled around with her flashlight until she found the house phone on her table. Keeping her eye on the fire, she dialed the front desk.

"Hello? Hello—this is Riley in the starfish room . . ."

"Riley?" It was Juliet. "Do you need a flashlight? There's one—"

"The tree outside my window is on fire! Some of the leaves landed on the balcony—the plants are burning . . ."

"Are you OK? I will call the fire department. How big are the flames by your room?"

Riley tried to stay calm. "Bigger than they were a second ago."

"OK, make sure your neighbors are up, right? Get them out in case it spreads. I'm on my way up."

Riley ran out the door. She shone her flashlight down the hall. All was quiet. Three doors. She pounded on the first. "Hey!" she yelled. "There's a fire. You've got to get out!"

Nadia opened the door, sleepy. "What?"

"My balcony's on fire. We're all getting out—go downstairs. In the living room unless they tell you something different down there."

She was on to the next one. The next. Two more sleepy women staggered down the hall. Riley hunted around. There had to be a fire extinguisher somewhere. She looked around the corner toward the staircase. There it was. She grabbed it, just as she heard footsteps on the stairs. Bob and Juliet came racing around the corner.

"In here!" Riley called. As they opened the door, the smoke smell grew stronger than before. Bob grabbed Riley's things and shoved her bag out into the hall.

"I think maybe we can get it," Juliet yelled. "The fire extinguisher . . ."

"I've got it!" Riley grabbed the nozzle. "If you open the door . . ."

Juliet did as told. Riley aimed the hose at the first burning plant and blasted the spray at it. Then the next one. Then the next one. They heard sirens in the distance, turning closer.

"Just in time," Bob called, racing back into the room. "Fire department is here."

Leaving Bob with the fire extinguisher to make sure everything was out, Juliet and Riley flew down the stairs, past the bewildered and pajama-clad women of MB huddled in the dark living room, and out the door just as a Maris fire engine parked on the street. "This way!" Juliet yelled as the men on duty surveyed the smoldering tree. One fireman cleared debris from the area. Another shone a giant flashlight at the scene. Two men aimed the hose just as a truck from a neighboring town wailed up too.

It wasn't a huge fire; within a few minutes, the flames were gone. A few plumes of smoke wafted up into the churning sky. Bob, with his flashlight, came back down to talk to the firemen about the property. Juliet brought Riley into the kitchen, where a backup generator was powering the refrigerator and a few lights. Using the gas stove and a match, Juliet whipped up a batch of hot chocolate for the fire crews. Riley helped distribute the marshmallows and carried the mugs outside. The rain had mostly stopped, but it was still drizzling enough that the men stood on the porch to sip from their mugs. "You know," one young man said, "this cocoa is really, really good . . . do you make this a lot? You could sell this stuff."

"Oh, I just dabble in the kitchen sometimes," Juliet said. One of the older men, who'd been in the area longer, threw his head back and laughed.

Their drinks finished, the crews waved, got back on their trucks, and drove down the road. As they disappeared into the deep lampless darkness, Juliet and Riley listened to the quietly dripping rain. Then, after a minute, they went back inside. Juliet fished around in a foyer drawer until she found a lighter. She lit three candles. Then she addressed the still-stunned women of MB, both those from Riley's floor and a handful of others awakened by the sirens.

"Well, I don't know about you, but I think I'd like something stronger than hot chocolate. What do you think?"

This was immediately agreed upon. Juliet fetched a few matching bottles from the cellar. She handed one to Nadia. Riley knew little about wine but everyone who'd been to Napa fawned over this particular merlot. Juliet grabbed ten glasses from the curio cabinet and twisted the cork out of one bottle. Nadia took a taste. She gave a thumbs-up. Perfect. In the candlelight, the dark red wine glowed with a memorable boldness. Riley looked down at a set of coasters on the coffee table. On them, in calligraphy: *You are always choosing.* They raised their glasses. They toasted that the fire hadn't damaged much.

"You know, Riley," Nadia teased, "I've been watching you run around since you banged on my door and you haven't checked your phone yet. I don't think I've ever seen you go half an hour before . . ."

"Oh!" Riley felt for her pocket, but she was wearing sweatpants. There weren't pockets. She actually had no idea where her phone was. In her room? Had Bob put it with her bag? She felt Juliet watching her. "Yes, well . . ." She paused. "When there's something more important to do, right? Infinite demands. Limited time . . ."

Juliet smiled. Her bracelet caught the light as she raised her glass to her lips.

Chapter 10

R iley woke later than she planned the next morning. She heard clangs, voices—the hum of her colleagues and the buzz of an espresso maker in the kitchen. She looked at the blinking alarm clock next to her. The power must have come back on. She sat up. Where was she? Sun streamed through the windows. One, facing the ocean, was cracked open, and a chill breeze ruffled her hair. The air held just a hint of smoke. She remembered: After the fire, after the late-night merlot, Bob had helped her move from the starfish room to a smaller room on the main floor. She forced herself out from under the warm down comforter and pulled on her now-dry jeans and a fleece before she could shiver. Drawn by the smell of coffee, she opened the door and slunk as quietly as she could on the creaky wood floor toward the common area.

"Well, if it isn't our firefighter!" Nadia said as Riley walked in, still blinking. The women of MB raised their mugs and cheered.

"Oh, please," Riley said.

"Fearlessly ignoring her email to evacuate the south wing and extinguish the burning bush!"

"Hear! Hear!" They clinked their mugs as Riley blushed and found an empty one, which she quickly filled. She hunted around for the cream. Real cream. The morning after envisioning stark choices for your future and putting out a fire called for something more fortifying than skim milk.

"Good morning, Riley," Juliet said. The sunlight streaming through the window glinted off her auburn hair. She stood back, radiant, as Betsy and Faye bustled around the kitchen. They plated eggs, bacon, and glistening, buttery biscuits served with little tins of jam made from strawberries the school grew on a farm a few miles inland. Juliet urged them all to visit for pick-your-own season in the summer. "Bob said the damage wasn't too bad. We'll be getting the tree service out here to get rid of those branches later today. And it's so nice this morning— warming up fast. You can eat outside if you want."

Riley didn't need to be convinced. Balancing a plate, and her coffee, and her silverware, she ambled off to the porch. She breathed in deeply as she sat down. All traces of the storm from the night before had vanished, save for seagulls swooping in to examine the detritus on the beach. The morning sun glittered off the calm sea. Juliet was right on the rising temperature; already the wind had changed from cold to pleasant. A few fishermen sat at the end of the pier. She could hear neighbors mopping up their porches. Someone shouted; a leaf blower hummed. The town of Maris was waking up. Morning brought everything back to normal. Even the fallen branches of the formerly flaming tree had been stacked neatly in a pile, testament to the efficient operations of Juliet's School of Possibilities. Down the street, a man parked a truck with a giant trailer. He climbed out and walked around to the back. As Riley ate her breakfast, he unloaded a dozen bicycles, one by one, onto the sidewalk.

She was lost in her thoughts when Juliet poked her head outside a few minutes later. "Sorry to rush you," she said, "but

I just talked to Tom, and he said that he's going to be ready to take you all on your boardwalk bike ride in just a bit."

"Oh." Riley took a big swig of her coffee. She answered by habit. "It sounds fun, but I should probably stay here and get my travel schedule sorted out for the week and . . ."

"*Really?* Really, Riley? *That's* what you'd choose to do over a lovely morning ride?"

"Well, when you put it that way . . ."

"Then . . ."

Riley laughed at herself and threw up her hands. As one of Juliet's acolytes whisked away her plate, Riley followed the small crowd of MB women in their weekend-warrior athletic garb down the street to grab a bike.

The man who was unloading them waved as they walked closer. And as they walked closer, Riley couldn't stop staring. He was tall. Almost unbelievably blond. Well-built, with a rugged face and deep blue eyes. He spoke with a slight accent as he introduced himself. "I'm Tom—I've been running Tom's Bikes, about three miles south from here, and leading rides for Juliet's guests since I moved from Copenhagen two years ago . . ."

Riley stifled a laugh. She couldn't help herself. Where was

Juliet? She whirled around, but the domestic maven had disappeared into her school somewhere. Riley had to admire the sheer audacity of her host's scheming as she recalled the description of her alleged future husband. Yes, Juliet did like to envision *all* possibilities.

Not that it would be a bad possibility. She had no idea what this man was like, but there on that storm-washed boardwalk, it didn't really matter. She was content to spend the next few hours replacing all thoughts of the word "challenges" in her head with glances at someone who was incredibly easy on the eyes.

The women of MB likewise whispered and twittered as they climbed on their bikes and followed Tom down the boardwalk. *I would have dressed nicer if I'd known. She just got our return business for next year, right, Nadia? Do you think we can ask for a chef who looks like him too?* The scenery, the joy of speed, made them buoyant. Autumn had mostly emptied the shore, and so they could fly down the smooth boards without needing to dodge clots of beach-goers. They could feel the cool wind waking them up as well as Juliet's espresso. Riley had pedaled toward the front of the line when Tom dropped back to bike beside her.

"So Juliet said you're the firefighter, right?"

She tried to decide if his eyes were closer to the color of the sea or the sky. "Oh, just a little excitement with the storm last night," she said. "Nothing major."

"Not in Juliet's telling. In her version you bravely rescued all your colleagues from their rooms and then rushed back toward the conflagration to single-handedly extinguish the flames."

"Is that what she told you?" Riley tried to picture Juliet calling her hunk of a neighbor to plant this idea. Always working her magic. "Just a little job with the fire extinguisher. I once put out a fire in my dorm in college, so I know the drill."

"Still." He glanced back toward the women of MB, stretched out over several hundred yards in groups of two to three. They were all watching him strike up a conversation with Riley. She hardly dared think about what teasing she was in for later. "I was on the volunteer fire crew back when I was in school. I know most people don't run toward flames."

"I see problems, and I try to solve them." It was true. It was what she had always wanted to do. It was the lure of MB—its promise that she could solve important problems and share those solutions on as big a stage as possible. For just a second, the image of Jean reading her performance review flashed into her brain. But she didn't want to let that cloud her thoughts now. She simply wanted to let her mind wander. She let herself float over the water, the beach houses, the autumn-bright trees.

"Do you like to bike?" Tom asked.

"I do, though I haven't . . ."

"I go on long rides most mornings before I lead tours. If you ever wanted to come along, I'd welcome company." He grinned and Riley couldn't help but smile back. Then Tom looked behind him at the train of women. "Oh, shoot, someone's stopped. OK, you all keep going! Down to the drawbridge. We'll catch up or meet you there!" He rode back to deal with the stuck gear or unaligned seat or whatever woe had befallen one of Riley's colleagues.

Riley kept pedaling. The morning shore was so beautiful she could think of little beyond the open sky. She breathed in the fresh, salty air. As she exhaled, her shoulders drifted down. Her jaw unclenched. She let her body revel in this strange sense. Was she . . . *relaxed*? She hadn't felt like this in a long time. Like all that was buzzing around her did not matter. Like she could see clearly. Like her brain was actually working as she flew away from the inbox dramas that could not matter in a year. She wasn't sure how to describe this openness. It felt exhilarating.

She pedaled faster, through a gust of wind that kicked up clouds of fallen scarlet leaves. She pondered how she might recount all this sand and sea and space to Skip. She recalled the vision of her friend beaming at the podium, and that happiness from decades hence made her happy. It made her happy right there. *Now.* She focused on that happiness. She wanted to see that happiness. She pondered how she might make that possible, how she might choose her minutes to make that vision come to be. She should call Skip more often. Meet her more often. Then she remembered Skip mentioning that her roommate was moving out soon. Riley's lease would be up in a few months. Maybe she should see if Skip would be up for sharing her place in Brooklyn. It was farther from the train station, and it might be harder to find a cab to the airport, but it would feel more like a home. She pictured herself walking through all those artisanal markets Juliet described, bringing groceries back to the kitchen in their Brooklyn home, where Skip would be fluttering about, telling tales of her middle school charges. She would like the companionship and . . .

Brooklyn. Home. Companion. In Riley's windswept brain, those three words caught on one another. She watched them stack up. Something came together. An image. A possibility.

Riley pedaled a little harder. As she thought about it, and thought through the logistics, it all began to make sense. She began to smile. And then she began to smile some more. The lighthouse loomed up ahead. *Oh, Skip.*

She might *finally* have an idea.

Chapter 11

T he *Brooklyn Home Companion*?" Skip asked.

Riley paced around her room, smoothing her white comforter as she talked on the phone, more excited than even she had imagined she might be. "Listen, Juliet said that people are obsessed with Brooklyn artisanal *anything*. Her daughters write blog posts about pickles, and page views go off the charts. You have your girls produce a magazine looking at crafts, food, urban farming, the arts. They can write poems and stories for it too, like those old *Woman's Home Companion* magazines. People love retro stuff. Anyway, the girls learn about writing and editing and graphics and publishing, and the business of producing a magazine, but the concept is about ten times more hip than your average school literary journal. People might actually read it, as opposed to a normal school publication. And you'd be positioning your nonprofit right in the center of this local scene."

"It sounds . . . intriguing."

"And listen, I mentioned it to Juliet because why not, right? I'm here. May as well try. And you know the first thing out of her mouth?"

"No."

"She said, 'I'd love to be an adviser. Do you think they'd want me? I'd be happy to help out.'"

"Oh my goodness. Um, yes."

"Yes, right? So do you think that's something your funder might like?"

"I think . . . there is a distinct possibility."

"You're meeting with her this afternoon, right?" Riley glanced at the alarm clock next to her bed. "Give me an hour, and I will send you a proposal."

Riley hung up and fished her laptop out of her bag. The women of MB were on a short break after biking so they could freshen up before their scrapbooking class. Riley figured she might be late to scrapbooking. She might not shower. She was fine with that choice. She glanced at the number on her inbox—1,459 unread messages—but so it went. There was only one email going out in the next hour that mattered to her anyway.

She felt a surge of energy as she sat down to work: the thrill of possibility at the start of any new project. *This* she knew how to do. If nothing else, MB had drilled her on the skill of turning a good idea into a compelling proposal. And this idea—which had sprung into her brain in a moment of utter clarity—would be unlike anything Skip's potential funder had seen. Riley tore through the Wikipedia entry on the *Woman's Home Companion*; she pulled up a quote from Gertrude Battles Lane, editor during the 1920s and 1930s heyday of the magazine. The reader "is forever seeking new ideas; I must keep her in touch with the best. Her horizon is ever extending, her interest broadening." *Just like Skip's girls.* Riley wrote up the skills they would learn. She threw in estimates on printing and distribution costs she'd learned through tangential research she'd done on a now-defunct People's Coffee Shops publication. She wrote about where the girls could distribute the magazine: the libraries, the craft fairs and maker spaces, the farming co-ops. She wrote a business plan for how the magazine could become self-sustaining after initial philanthropic support. And then she doubled down on the print aspect of it. Of course, everything was online these days. But the whole point of the Brooklyn artisanal scene was going back to real things, enabled by technology, but also slightly apart from it.

Also, Juliet was willing to put her name on the masthead. So there was that.

She finished a draft in forty-five minutes, then spent the next fifteen minutes editing. She marveled at her own execution. She sent the document to Skip.

A few minutes later, Skip replied with a text message full of emoji hearts.

So she was being put in Challenges, Riley thought. She knew she was good at this. The powers that reigned at MB could suggest her resignation. They could change their euphemism and *demand* it. She would be fine. She loved finding problems and solving them, and when she needed to work, she could work harder than anyone else. She was always choosing, and this work was her calling. This work was where she worked her magic, and when she focused on what she could do best, she could see what others couldn't.

That opened up all sorts of possibilities.

Chapter 12

Later that afternoon, the women of MB oohed and ahhed over one another's scrapbooks. These keepsakes did indeed look fabulous, albeit thanks to staff help every bit as intensive as they'd received with the meringue the night before.

Riley, on the other hand, though fifteen minutes late to class, had spent the remaining time grilling every staff member in the room about page layout techniques, fonts, and complementary material textures. Maybe she'd volunteer with Skip's girls sometime. If she was going into the magazine business, she needed to understand more about aesthetics than one might assume from her navy and charcoal suit rotation.

She kept pondering the *Brooklyn Home Companion* as she worked. Skip had liked her proposal enough that Riley jotted down notes of backup plans: a dozen other potential funders if this first one didn't bite, and people she knew who worked at each of those places, so she could introduce Skip and get her meetings. She showed her colleagues her book of autumn photos, and smiled through a presentation from Jean on MB's new training programs. But then as people drifted up to pack, she wandered off on her own. She snapped pictures of Juliet's school, and the beach, and the boardwalk. The cawing birds, flying south, filled her with a sense of openness. Maybe she'd try a scrapbook of the weekend. Or just a few pages with those words to remind her: *Expectations are infinite. Time is finite. You are always choosing. Choose well.* She couldn't quite explain it, but every time she repeated that phrase, the words seemed to push her on to try new things.

She finally made her way back, her mind settling down to earth as the sun tilted behind the trees, heralding the arrival of late afternoon. Riley's colleagues gathered for one more round of fizzy drinks. They toasted their newfound domestic prowess before they summoned their car services to go home, or in some cases, to Newark airport for Sunday-night flights to Europe. Those 9 a.m. meetings in London, Paris, and Frankfurt beckoned. Such was the MB pace. You learned not to leave home without your passport.

Riley, likewise, had her passport in her bag, but her colleagues' departures found her still standing on the porch, looking out at the ocean. She was not quite ready to leave this place. She was still standing there when her phone buzzed. Should she ignore it? Then she looked at the name.

Elsa.

Quite odd—most likely a mistaken dial from someone who'd expressed doubts about ever speaking to her again. But she picked it up nonetheless.

"Elsa, this is Riley Jenkins. Did you mean to call me?"

"Oh yes, sorry to disturb your Sunday . . ." Riley let that thought go unanswered. Elsa knew full well that when you hired MB, weekends were fair game. "Anyway, I wanted to talk with you because, well, it seems we know someone in common. Skip."

"Oh—you know Skip?"

"*You* can't talk about your clients without their permission. *She* can't talk about potential funders who ask to be anonymous in the exploration process but *I* can be a loudmouth and talk to you both. Anyway, PCS was looking to invest in a few philanthropic ventures and I'd happened to meet her at a party a few months ago . . ."

"So you were . . ." *That* party?

"Today she showed me the proposal for the *Brooklyn Home Companion*. I thought she was brilliant." Riley took in a deep breath. She started to answer, but Elsa kept going. "Let me just tell you, I never see such business-minded proposals from the nonprofit people I meet with. Even those with professional grant writers. They'll save the world, but they don't think about how sustainable their ventures might be if they can't keep fundraising . . . Anyway, she freely confessed that her friend Riley Jenkins, management consultant extraordinaire, was the brains behind the operation."

Riley blushed. She walked to the other end of the porch and leaned on the railing as she watched a small crew launch a boat from the dock. "Oh, you know, I just helped her sharpen the idea."

"No, she said it was *your* idea. And she said that you were the one who convinced Juliet to come on board as an adviser. I don't think I have to tell you how excited I would be to be associated with her on something like this."

Riley pulled herself together. *Focus on the desired outcome.*

"Well, if you've outed yourself, I hope you don't mind me lobbying you to consider funding the proposal. Skip is amazing, and her girls really deserve to be given more opportunities and . . ."

"You can stop, Riley. I already told her she's good. Heck, if it's good enough, we might distribute it in our shops. I mean, we've needed something since our own in-house publication didn't pan out."

"Well . . . well . . . that's wonderful. I'm thrilled. Thank you. I think you'll be proud of what they do."

"I also want to apologize. I recall that yesterday—was that yesterday?—I may have complained about your lack of interesting ideas." Riley sat on one of the rocking chairs. Yes, that had only been yesterday. "I don't know what happened with that proposal you all sent me Friday, but maybe we can chat again. Maybe we just weren't hearing each other. I'm sure if you and I chat a bit more we can come up with some good stuff that you and MB could do for PCS. Right?"

"Of course," Riley said. "Of course."

Chapter 13

When Juliet came out on the porch a few minutes later, Riley was still sitting on the rocking chair. She was staring at her phone, but looked up as a truck rumbled down the street. She saw Juliet watching her. "Are you *still* cleaning out your inbox?" Juliet shook her head and adjusted the leaf wreath on the door.

"Oh no, just some logistics." Riley stood up and put her phone in her pocket. "I was heading out to my car in a minute. But guess what. I heard from the client who dumped me."

"Yes?"

"Turns out—she said I could tell you this—that she was the funder meeting with my friend. They agreed to fund the *Brooklyn Home Companion,* and she was so excited about it—and about your being an adviser for it—that she wanted me to come meet with her and talk about other ideas I might have. So . . . thank you. For saving my career."

"Oh, Riley. I only say yes to what I really want to do. Can you believe I might be as excited as you are about this project?" Juliet retrieved a few stray cushions and straightened the seashells displayed on a table. "And as for other possibilities, I suspect that you and MB might find ways—might *keep* finding ways—to stay happy with each other."

"Yes. I told my client I'd come see her for a good long discussion on Tuesday."

Juliet paused, conch shell in hand. "*Tuesday?* In my mind, Riley Jenkins is more of a show-up-on-Monday-morning sort of person."

"Yes, but expectations are infinite. Time is finite," Riley said. "I just made myself a hotel reservation for tonight at a place a mile from here. My client wants good ideas, and it seems I get good ideas while biking, so . . ." Her eyes twinkled. "I want to go on a really, *really* long bike ride first thing tomorrow morning."

"Oh!" Juliet laughed and put the shell back on the table. "Imagine that! A bike ride? Just for ideas? Or perhaps with . . . company?"

"Perhaps," Riley said with a smile. "But *that* is my top priority for the day. Here's hoping I'm choosing well."

The Power of Priorities

A GUIDE TO

SPENDING MORE TIME ON WHAT MATTERS,

AND LESS ON WHAT DOESN'T

by

Laura Vanderkam

F or years, I've been studying people's schedules and helping them figure out how to make time for their priorities. I wrote *Juliet's School of Possibilities* because I know that sometimes stories make concepts more memorable than straightforward instructions.

Thank you for making the time to read this parable. I know that expectations are infinite, and time is finite. I know you are busy. I appreciate your choosing to make reading this story a priority in your life.

I hope Riley Jenkins's transformation inspires you to think

about your own future, and how you can make choices with your time to turn that vision into reality. The exercises in this guide will help you think about how you spend your time, and how you'd like to spend your time.

First, let's look forward.

In her weekend at Juliet's School of Possibilities, Riley Jenkins envisions a future where she is both professionally and personally fulfilled. She is having a positive impact on the broader world.

Carve out some quiet time and picture yourself a few years in the future. Because Riley is so young, her vision took her a few decades into the future; those of us who are older don't need to go nearly so far. But create a picture of yourself at this future time. You feel happy and relaxed. You are spending your time in purposeful ways. Make this picture as vivid as possible. Where are you? Who is with you? How do you spend your weekdays? Your weekends?

Now think about these people who are with you. Picture them celebrating you for the impact you've had on them and the world. Think about a toast, or a speech they might give. What would they say? As you think about this celebratory speech, list the major examples of professional and personal impact here:

_____

_____

_____

_____

_____

_____

_____

_____

_____

_____

_____

_____

_____

_____

_____

_____

_____

_____

_____

Now we can move toward the more immediate future.

On the professional front, picture yourself at the end of the next calendar year. You are giving yourself a professional performance review. It is a great review, because it has been a great year. You have made major advances toward the future goals you listed earlier. What three things did you do during the year that made it so amazing?

1. _____

   _____

   _____

   _____

2. _____

_____

_____

_____

_____

3. _____

_____

_____

_____

You can do this for your personal life too. Picture yourself at the end of the next calendar year. You are a guest at a holiday party. You are happily recounting your previous year for friends and family. The reason for such happiness? It has been an amazing year for you and the people you care about. You have made steady progress toward the vision of your future you created earlier. What three things did you do during the year that made it so amazing?

1. _____

_____

_____

2. _____

3. _____

Over the next few months, these six year-end goals should inform your scheduling choices. Think about the next week. What steps could you take toward each of these goals?

Where could you put these steps in your schedule?

How will you hold yourself accountable for achieving them?

_____

_____

_____

_____

_____

_____

_____

_____

_____

_____

_____

_____

As you ponder your priorities, I think it's helpful to figure out where the time really goes *now*. Having a clear sense of your schedule will help you make smart choices.

The best way to figure out where the time goes is to track your time for a week. Here is a picture of a time log breaking the 168-hour week into half-hour blocks. To track your time on such a log, you would write down what you're doing, checking in three to four times per day to fill in what you've done since the last check-in. Broad categories are OK—work, sleep, drive, make dinner, play with kids—because consistency is more important than documenting every single minute.

If you would like a larger Excel or PDF version of this log, please visit my website, LauraVanderkam.com, and fill out the subscription form so I can email you one.

	Monday	Tuesday	Wednesday	Thursday	Friday	Saturday	Sunday
5 A.M.							
5:30							
6							
6:30							
7							
7:30							
8							
8:30							
9							
9:30							
10							
10:30							
11							
11:30							
12 P.M.							
12:30							
1							
1:30							
2							
2:30							
3							
3:30							
4							
4:30							
5							
5:30							
6							
6:30							
7							
7:30							
8							
8:30							
9							
9:30							
10							
10:30							
11							
11:30							
12 A.M.							
12:30							
1							
1:30							
2							
2:30							
3							
3:30							
4							
4:30							

After you have tracked your time, ask yourself a few questions about your schedule:

1. What do I like most about my time?

2. What do I want to spend more time doing?

3. What would I like to spend less time doing?

4. What steps can I take to make those changes?

I would love to hear what you discover! You can email me at laura@lauravanderkam.com.

Group Discussion Questions

How we choose to spend time affects everyone around us. If you've read *Juliet's School of Possibilities* with your team or with other members of a professional or social organization, you can gather in small groups (ideally four to eight people) to discuss these questions.

- On the way to her retreat, Riley realizes she has disappointed the people who are closest to her, personally and professionally. Have you (or anyone in the group) ever dropped the ball when you felt overwhelmed? As you look back on this experience, what circumstances led to this situation of feeling overwhelmed? What did you decide to do differently as a result?

■ Riley's particular weakness was trying to respond to all emails instantly, but many activities can consume more time than people like. As you think about how you and your team spend your time, what activities take more hours and energy than you think they're worth? Why do you think they consume so much time?

■ If you could spend an additional hour on one professional activity per week, what would it be?

■ If you could spend an additional hour on one personal activity per week, what would it be?

■ Where do you think you might make time in your schedule for these activities? When are other people in the discussion group making time for these activities?

- Juliet reminds Riley that she is always choosing how to spend her time, and so she should choose well. Think back to a time when you had to make a tough choice, or your team had to make a tough choice, about how to spend time. What did you decide to do? What were the ramifications?

- Have you ever needed to disappoint someone's immediate expectation in order to meet a larger one? How did you handle the situation? What was the outcome?

- Riley dreams up her career-saving idea while she's biking along the boardwalk. Where and when do you get your best ideas? Think back to a recent mental breakthrough. How did that idea come to you? What were the circumstances, and how could they be replicated?

- Have you ever had an opportunity come to you when you changed how you spent your time?

- Looking forward to next week, what one change would you like to make in your schedule to make more time for your priorities?

■ Who in the group can hold you accountable for this change?

■ Check back one week later. Did you make the change to your schedule? If so, what made that change possible? If you didn't make the change to your schedule, why not? How could you address these challenges?